A Cautionary Tale on the Perils
of Having No Plan for Board Development

Susan, who runs a successful small business, is approached by a
friend who asks her to join the board of a local nonprofit
dedicated to providing short-term shelter and extensive follow-
up services to troubled adolescents in the community. Her
initial instinct is to decline; she is busy at work and involved in
a renovation project at home. But this is the first time she has
been invited to serve on a board, and as Susan listens to her
friend describe the organization, a little of his enthusiasm rubs
off. It is time for her to work on something other than her own
concerns. Susan accepts the invitation and notes the board's
next meeting on her calendar.

▼

U
nless they have founded the organization, most people
serve on the board of a nonprofit because they are
invited. Sometimes the invitation is a result of careful
research and consideration; other times, as with Susan, it is the
product of a more casual recruitment process. People say yes for
a combination of reasons—most highly laudable, some less so.
The primary reason is usually a personal commitment to the
organization's mission. People may also have skills that the
nonprofit can use and that they are willing to share, or they
may feel they can bring a perspective that will help shape
programs and services. They may also be flattered to be asked
and discover that flattery of this kind is hard to resist.

Whatever their reasons, people usually join a board with
enough interest and good will to make a credible contribution
to it and the organization. Of the thousands of board members
the National Center for Nonprofit Boards (NCNB) has met,
served, and advised, not one has announced when joining a
board an intention to do a poor job. But even doing the best
you can means little if board members, individually and
collectively, have no clear sense of what the work of governing a
nonprofit entails and are given little opportunity to learn.

1

"Board development" is a catchall phrase that describes the many large and small activities that can provide board members with opportunities to learn—about the organization and its purpose, about the board's role and how it is best fulfilled, about themselves and the staff as members of a team, and about the people or communities they serve.

Board development also means helping boards put their work for particular organizations into the larger context of nonprofit work generally. What does the law require? What are the standards of practice in a particular field or in the nonprofit community at large? How have other organizations approached this issue or solved this problem?

Board development can involve distinct events, such as retreats and workshops organized to explore particular topics, or a larger commitment to view the board as an asset—one that benefits, like buildings and equipment, from proper use and an investment in careful maintenance.

This booklet outlines a broad strategy for continuous development of the board and suggests activities that help boards focus on their roles and responsibilities as stewards of the organizations they serve.

The cautionary tale continues:

At her first board meeting, Susan is formally welcomed to the board, introductions are made around the table, and business begins. She keeps her ears open and volunteers to assist on a special event that is being planned. She notices that discussion of a few issues drags on without resolution and that some disagreements appear to be habitual. In the course of the discussion, a number of board members tune out, leaving the chair to find a way to move the agenda along. By the time the financial report is tackled, people are looking at their watches, and several interesting questions are referred to the staff to look into and report back on.

When Susan asks her colleague about the board's lack of focus and the tension she sensed between some board members, he sighs and rolls his eyes. He explains that the board is at an awkward stage. Several founding board members remain and are having a hard time adjusting to changes in the organization. A new executive director has just been hired and has ruffled a few feathers by deciding a couple of matters that his predecessor routinely took to the board for approval. Moreover, the chair is new and not as dynamic or assertive as she needs to be. None of this matters, he assures Susan. This is a great organization, and its work is a real contribution to the community.

Think of the board of a nonprofit as a boat full of people trying to reach land. Three things will determine their success: their skill as sailors, the integrity of the vessel, and the body of water in which they find themselves.

If the sailors are skilled but the boat is in poor repair, keeping it afloat will be a struggle, but not impossible if the water remains relatively calm. If the sailors lack skill and experience, they may reach land, but only if the boat is sound and all other circumstances are in their favor. A little turbulence or a small leak, and both boat and crew may be sunk.

Oher scenarios spring to mind: an organization becalmed while the board argues about whose job it is to row; an organization full of leaks while the board argues about whose job it is to see to repairs; an organization adrift while the board debates the way to terra firma. All these situations are easy to envision if the board has been enlisted without skills or the chance to master them.

OBSTACLES TO BOARD DEVELOPMENT

The first obvious question to ask is, Why have these people set out with so little expertise or preparation? Why do so many boards struggle to find a way to work with each other and with the staff to further the success of the organization? To answer this question requires a frank look at the obstacles to board development.

It takes time, and time is always at a premium. Board members are volunteers, giving up personal time to be involved. Executive directors and staff have barely enough time to meet the day-to-day demands of their jobs. For board and staff, there is always more to do than board meetings and committee meetings reasonably allow. Who has time to spend a day attending a workshop or assessing the board's role in the organization?

It takes initiative and leadership. The issue of responsibility for board development is discussed later, but if the board chair is indifferent to the idea, there is little that can overcome that inertia. If the executive director fails to perceive the benefits of a better informed board, or worries about what a more effective board might mean to the status quo, board development is likely to be last on a long list of things to do.

It may cost money, and there is never enough of that. Although much board development can be achieved at no financial cost, some very effective board development activities require a budget. To help the board succeed in a new fund-raising endeavor, for example, board members and staff may need to call on outside expertise. Retreats often benefit from the use of an outside facilitator to guide discussions and to serve as an interested, but unbiased, observer and participant. In addition, the cost of attending professional meetings and workshops that would benefit board members may need to be part of the nonprofit's budget if board members cannot handle such costs themselves.

It takes modesty. To learn anything requires admitting to a little ignorance or room for improvement. Board members often find it hard to accept that the skills and personal characteristics that made them attractive as potential board members— expertise, single-mindedness, entrepreneurship, influence—may present a challenge to effective board service, in which working as a team, reaching consensus, respecting boundaries, and putting other people or organizations first play a part in success.

Last, who knew there was so much to learn? Board members are often surprised to learn that they have legal obligations as members of a nonprofit board and that consequently they have some inescapable responsibilities, including fiscal oversight, careful attention to program activities, and evaluation of staff performance. In addition, going from work in the for-profit world to work as a volunteer on a nonprofit board, or from one nonprofit board to another, is not always a smooth transition. Nonprofits have a distinctive legal structure and culture, and whatever the similarities among nonprofits, each has its own history and organizational imperative that define the role of the board.

Finally, although the situation is beginning to change, the literature on governance in the nonprofit sector is not widely known to board members. Unlike business or health, nonprofit governance doesn't have its own section in the local bookstore. As professionals and members of the community, board members may read in their field or keep up with civic events through the newspaper, but only the most diligent are likely to find—much less spend time with—the growing body of material on nonprofit governance.

WHOSE JOB IS IT?

Good board development does not happen by magic. It needs to be viewed as a task or a series of tasks that must be assigned if they are ever to be completed.

Board development is a shared responsibility of the executive director, the board chair, and the board as a whole. The executive director is responsible for encouraging the board to seek opportunities to learn what they need to be effective and for helping to identify and structure activities that enable the board to achieve that goal. The board chair should provide leadership and a good example by making opportunities during the board's scheduled work to accommodate events or discussions that help the board strengthen its performance, and by personally participating in these activities. The board as a whole must be open to opportunities to learn and make itself available when these activities are scheduled.

Executive directors or development officers of organizations often take the initiative to introduce opportunities for board development, both because they have ready access to information about governance-related resources and because their success is often linked to the board's performance. The board should welcome rather than resist these efforts. The staff alone cannot make the board improve its performance; the board must be a willing partner.

To focus attention on governance matters, boards often create special committees on governance or board affairs. These committees usually are charged with helping identify and recruit new members, evaluating current members, and identifying and arranging opportunities for board development activities, such as retreats. In some organizations, there may be a staff person assigned to work directly on board affairs. This person supports the executive director and the board chair in managing board business.

However, creating a specially charged board committee or assigning staff to work with the board does not relieve the executive director and the board chair of their responsibility to lead and support ongoing board development. Indifference, inertia, or unwillingness to see effective governance as something that needs to be nurtured create insurmountable obstacles to board development.

Those who know enough to appreciate the complexity of board service are prime candidates for board development. They have met the first condition of effective board development: a willingness to learn. In addition to that critical piece of good will, other elements are necessary to successful boards and successful board development.

BOARD COMPOSITION AND RECRUITMENT

An overarching consideration in any plan for developing the board should be attention to who serves on it. Even if a board is appointed or elected through a formula that defines its composition, some standards for participation should be developed.

Have members been identified carefully for the skills and energy they can bring to board service? Many invitations are extended to friends and colleagues because it is easier to work within a small, comfortable circle than to approach strangers who may slow things down or rock an already unsteady boat. Often new board members are enticed to serve with the promise "It won't take much time, and you won't have to raise money." The result is a board filled with people who (surprise!) do not give enough time and cannot be depended on for financial support.

Look at the current strengths of the board, consider where the organization is and where it needs to go, and then decide

DRAFTING A JOB DESCRIPTION
FOR BOARD MEMBERS

In conjunction with a self-assessment, the board of the Sex Information and Education Council of the United States (SIECUS) developed the following summary of the board's role and the qualities of a board member. Among the qualities of a board member, they listed the following:

- Expertise
- Being a team player
- Judgment/experience
- Time for board service
- Commitment/caring
- Loyalty
- Flexibility
- Support for/belief in the mission

The job description for a SIECUS board member follows:

As a SIECUS board member, you will be expected to actively participate in the functions of the SIECUS board:

1. Support the mission.
2. Attend board meetings and actively participate in decision-making.
3. Read written materials in preparation for board meetings and decision-making.
4. Share your particular areas of expertise with the board and staff.
5. Be an advocate for the organization; promote SIECUS in ways appropriate to your profession and contacts.
6. Maintain SIECUS membership, and, in addition to membership, make a financial contribution appropriate to your circumstances.

Reproduced with the permission of SIECUS.

what kind of people should be at the table. Don't be reluctant to describe the time, effort, and dedication it takes to be a successful board member. If the current board works hard (or needs to work harder), make this clear to those being recruited. Don't sell the board's work short.

Develop a job description. Develop a recruitment plan. Don't let the nominating committee be the poor relation of board work. It should be the most important committee of the board, helping to guide the full board through the critical process of creating dynamic and continuous volunteer leadership for the organization.

ORIENTATION

Board development should begin with a strong orientation program for new board members that draws on the energy, expertise, and interests of the staff, the board chair, and the board as a whole. A strong orientation program sets a standard for work on the board. It lets people begin to contribute as quickly as possible and communicates how important it is to start off fully informed and ready to participate.

Sending new members an indigestible wad of literature about the organization and introducing them briefly at their first board meeting is like tossing out a life preserver with too short a rope. Don't begin a working relationship by asking people to paddle desperately toward you for six months to a year. They may catch up, but they are just as likely to give up in frustration.

An orientation program ensures that board members are reading from the same page. If they are left to form their own interpretations of the mission, it should be no surprise if board members develop conflicting theories, making it difficult to reach agreement when resources are allocated or planning is undertaken. Similarly, board members unfamiliar with the quality and variety of programs an organization offers will find it hard to constructively evaluate the performance of the organization and the staff.

Besides having practical advantages, a thorough orientation is a courtesy that current board members extend to their new colleagues, making them feel welcome and allowing them to join the board's discussions and decision making with confidence.

Create opportunities before the first board meeting for new members to meet the executive director and learn something about the programs firsthand. Match new members with experienced board members who can serve as personal guides to the board and its business, providing background information about the current members and reviewing the agenda of the first meeting to give the context for certain items of business and to answer questions.

If the first few board meetings will include information or decisions of a technical nature—the annual budget or a government grant or contract—arrange a special pre-meeting orientation and refresher session for new and current board members. This session can serve as an introduction to the special body of knowledge or vocabulary board members must have to comprehend the issues, ask good questions, and provide approval or useful guidance.

For boards whose members must travel a long distance to attend meetings, the pre-meeting session may be the only option for face-to-face orientation. Distance is a challenge, not an obstacle, to a good orientation.

SELF-ASSESSMENT

At the other end of the spectrum of board development is board self-assessment. Self-assessments are a way for board members to step back from the relentless nature of most board meetings and reflect on the performance and effectiveness of the board. Regular board meetings usually do not permit members to stop as each piece of business is concluded and ask themselves how well or poorly they went about the process of making decisions. Board members have no chance to scrutinize their discussions to see whether the tenor and content of the discussions reflected a good sense of the relative responsibilities of board and staff.

A board self-assessment gives a board the opportunity to explore those and other issues in a way that is both constructive and affirming for the organization. NCNB's experience with board self-assessment has repeatedly reinforced the value of the process for successful boards and for boards struggling to clarify issues relating to their work or the larger work of the organization.

A good self-assessment requires:

◆ An effective questionnaire or other tool for eliciting information from the board;

◆ A process that allows board members to be candid without fear of awkwardness or of compromising themselves;

◆ A report that summarizes the board's responses; and

◆ A meeting for exploring the results and deciding on ways to improve the board's performance as a whole.

NCNB has developed a questionnaire that focuses on the basic areas of responsibility for most boards. To each set of questions, board members can provide straightforward "satisfied" and "dissatisfied" responses and also suggest ways the board might strengthen its performance in a particular area. Because the confidentiality of each member's responses is respected, the observations and suggestions that board members share are a rich source of ideas for clarifying the board's thinking and identifying strategies for increasing the board's effectiveness.

The key to an effective self-assessment is the commitment to review and act on the results. The review typically takes place at a special board meeting at which enough time has been set aside for a full discussion of the issues that emerge. The board may choose to hold a retreat or to dedicate part of a regular board meeting to consider the results.

To guarantee a good response to the questionnaire and strong attendance at the meeting at which the results will be reviewed, self-assessments must be well planned and placed on the calendar far enough in advance to ensure the full board's participation.

Although a board self-assessment can be conducted entirely by a board using its own resources and tapping a member to guide the discussion, most boards find it more productive to use an outside facilitator—either a consultant or a board member from another organization with experience in facilitating governance-related discussions.

The use of a third party makes possible a more objective review of the results as well as a more thorough and organized discussion. It may also require the investment of funds to pay for a consultant's time or travel expenses.

A board self-assessment is not an annual event; most boards should consider undertaking a self-assessment only every few years. Moreover, self-assessment may not be appropriate in all situations. Boards with many new members may find that there is not enough experience to assess. Although boards that are about to engage in strategic planning may find self-assessment a useful starting point, boards that have just adopted a strategic or long-range plan may find self-assessment at that point to be of marginal value.

Self-assessment is also not a process for boards facing crises. While it might be useful to discover how the board could have avoided a major financial shortfall, the immediate necessity of resolving the crisis makes reflection difficult, if not superfluous.

Similarly, if the relationship between the chief executive and the board is strained, the purpose of the self-assessment can easily be subverted if board members see the opportunity to be candid only as a convenient way to vent their feelings about the executive.

OTHER BOARD DEVELOPMENT ACTIVITIES

Between an orientation session and a board self-assessment are a wealth of other possible board development activities.

Review the organization's mission. For many boards, the mission is a sentence or two in the organization's publications or a paragraph in the orientation materials. Missions need to be revisited periodically; they are not static. The environment in which an organization operates often changes, presenting new opportunities or making ongoing activities obsolete. The board

REVISITING THE MISSION

Missions need to be reaffirmed and sometimes revised. Revisiting the mission is a useful exercise for board development and an essential part of any long-range planning process. To help get a discussion going, ask the board the following questions:

- ◆ How would you describe the mission of the organization? (Board members should write descriptions individually and then compare theirs with those of other board members. This exercise assumes that the current mission statement is not posted in the room or written at the top of the page in front of them.)
- ◆ Is the current mission statement appropriate for the organization's role in the next two to four years?
- ◆ Does the board's decision-making on policies and program matters reflect the mission?

Regardless of the answers to these questions, the next question is always, How can the board do better in this area?

Adapted from *Self-Assessment for Nonprofit Governing Boards* by Larry H. Slesinger, published by the National Center for Nonprofit Boards.

has the primary responsibility to establish the mission of the organization and uphold it. Decisions should be tested against the mission. It is not enough to assume that everyone on the board understands the mission and how to use it to make decisions, evaluate programs, and chart a course for the future. Reviewing the mission and discussing its relevance enables board members to renew their commitment to the organization and express their feelings about the value of the work they support.

Organize board training workshops. Sometimes boards need specific training and education programs, particularly in fund-raising, financial accountability, and legal liability. Board members find it hard to be successful if they are asked to help raise funds for the first time without adequate preparation. Even board members with fund-raising experience may find it difficult to make the shift from an annual campaign to an endowment or capital campaign without preparation and planning.

A similar investment in training may be required to make board members comfortable with the organization's financial reporting system or with the annual audit. And in a litigious environment, board members may need outside experts to help them understand volunteer protection laws, risk management, and state and federal employment laws that affect personnel policies.

Plan retreats. Boards often use retreats for long-range planning or a thorough review of programs and finances. A retreat is typically an opportunity for board and staff to build stronger relationships with each other. For board members in particular, it offers unusual opportunities to get to know one another better and build camaraderie and good will. Retreats require good planning to be successful and need to respect the temperament and working style of the board. Some boards embrace the opportunity to use retreats to encourage closer

FOOLPROOFING RETREATS

Board retreats are a major investment of board and staff time and, if an outside facilitator is hired, a major investment of money as well. Nothing succeeds like success, and if you ever hope to persuade the board to hold another retreat, good planning is key. Avoid these mistakes:

◆ The goals of the retreat are too broad or too vague.

◆ The agenda is one presentation after another, with little or no time for discussion.

◆ The selection of goals, topics, and speakers reflects what one person thinks the board *ought* to know.

◆ The board is not consulted in the planning of the retreat.

◆ The speaker, facilitator, or facility was not carefully screened in advance.

◆ The time and place were ill suited to the board members' preferences and availability.

Adapted from *Planning Successful Board Retreats: A Guide for Board Members and Chief Executives* by Barry S. Bader, published by the National Center for Nonprofit Boards.

relationships among board members; others may be more comfortable with a "cooler," more businesslike agenda.

In addition to good planning, retreats need good attendance by board members to accomplish their board development purposes. Agree on a date well in advance, and repeatedly remind people to keep the date open.

Focus on problems in governance. Is the committee structure inoperative? Is the board recruitment process stale? Is the board diverse enough to exert strong and credible leadership in the organization and the community? Are board meetings well organized? too frequent? not frequent enough? too long? Discussion of these and other issues makes excellent use of two to three hours of a board's time. To make the best use of these opportunities, plan the discussions carefully. Simply raising an issue has limited value if what is really required is a clear agreement to move the issue toward change or resolution.

Broaden board members' horizons. Although some board members have professional expertise related to the missions of the organizations they serve, many do not. Giving board members opportunities to learn about the broader context in which an organization works is a valuable service. Board members can benefit from knowing what trends are shaping the field in which the organization works or shaping or reshaping the community in which it operates. Use senior staff for this purpose, or invite speakers from government, academia, or sister agencies to share research and information with the board. Such education enhances the board's ability to engage in strategic decision making and evaluate current programs.

Attend workshops offered by management assistance organizations. In many communities, a nonprofit management assistance provider—such as the United Way, the Support Center, or a community foundation—offers workshops tailored to the interests and needs of board members. NCNB offers a series of workshops around the country on a variety of governance-related topics. Individual board members who can make time to attend such workshops should consider making use of these resources. Although a workshop organized for a general audience of board members does not enable the full board to work together on issues specific to their organization, the workshops do provide a way for individual board members to accumulate ideas and strategies that might be adapted for the full board, and they give board members from a cross section of organizations in a community a chance to meet and exchange ideas and information.

The cautionary tale concludes:

Over the two years Susan serves on the board, she sees how important the organization is to troubled young people in the community. The kids, the staff, and the volunteers are all special. What is less special is the board. The problems she saw at the first meeting are never resolved and only grow worse. Two or three board members are now openly antagonistic. Important opportunities are lost because the board can't reach agreement. More upsetting is the increasing lack of confidence in the executive director. He is a competent man with energy and drive, but the board second-guesses every decision, magnifying problems and only grudgingly acknowledging success. Although Susan spends her first year on the board looking for ways to contribute and make herself useful, she finds more and more reasons to miss meetings and prays for a speedy conclusion to those she does attend.

When the chair of the nominating committee approaches her at the end of her term, Susan is astonished to be asked to consider chairing the board. She was contemplating a graceful resignation, not a deeper level of involvement.

As Susan thinks about the offer, she comes to view it as symptomatic of the board's underlying problems. She knows that she has not been an exemplary member over the last nine months. Offering her the position of chair is another example of the quick-fix, grasp-at-straws strategy that has enabled the board to avoid solving its fundamental problems.

Susan to the rescue! It is a tempting and highly flattering image, but one she finally rejects. The board needs to spend more time focusing on itself and how to strengthen its contribution to the organization and less time managing the organization's already well-managed day-to-day affairs. Susan cannot see herself convincing others on the board of the wisdom or the necessity of a thorough self-scrutiny. With a few suggestions of other candidates who have the temperament and skills to be chair and a pledge of continuing financial support for the organization, Susan tenders her resignation.

According to McDonald's corollary to Murphy's law, in any set of circumstances the proper course of action is determined by subsequent events. Looking back, Susan can see what steps would have created a better board, a stronger program, and a more rewarding and productive personal experience. Did anyone on the board deliberately choose to be ineffective or incompetent? No. Instead, the board chair, the executive director, and the board members were guilty of grave sins of omission. The board chair failed to exert the necessary leadership; the executive director was too embattled to see the board as a resource rather than an encumbrance; and most significant, other members of the board sat and watched, preferring to resign rather than speak up for a better approach to governance.

Over the years, the nonprofit sector has invested in increasing the management capacity of its employees. It is now possible, for instance, to study the management of nonprofits as part of a master's program in business, or to earn a degree or certificate in a specialized field such as arts management. In every major city in the country, one can find an array of courses that enable nonprofit staff to become more adept at the tasks necessary for successful management of a nonprofit organization.

Board members must struggle to get access to a comparable level of educational opportunity. Most boards must build their own boat. A plan for learning about and developing good governance must be tailored by the board itself, drawing on many sources—experience with other boards and other organizations, the interest and willingness of the staff, and the literature on effective governance.

Board development often occurs only when boards face difficulties or impasses that undermine organizations' ability to move forward. At NCNB, one goal is to remove some of the mystery and the burden of creating effective board development, which is part organized activity, part state of mind. The board and staff of a nonprofit organization should view board development as a natural outgrowth of a board's desire to do its best for the organization and the community it is trying to serve.

A good board and a good board development program share the same foundations. Putting together a good board takes time, commitment, and leadership. Once assembled, a good board deserves the investment of time, commitment, and leadership needed to keep it that way.

APPENDIX A:
HOW TO CONSTRUCT BETTER
BOARD MEETINGS

Attendance spotty? Attention flagging? The reasons may be readily obtained from board members themselves. Try administering the following questionnaire periodically at the end of board meetings. The collated responses could be used by the chief executive and board chair to plan future meetings, or shared with the board for further discussion.

The issues we covered today were:
Trivial   1 2 3 4 5   Essential

The materials provided were:
Worthless   1 2 3 4 5   Indispensable

Today's discussion concerned primarily:
Operations   1 2 3 4 5   Policy & Strategy

What might we have done differently to improve our meeting today?

What was the most valuable contribution we made to the organization's welfare today?

In light of today's meeting, what are the most important topics we should address at our next meeting?

Adapted from *How to Help Your Board Govern More and Manage Less* by Richard P. Chait, published by the National Center for Nonprofit Boards.

APPENDIX B:
BOARD DEVELOPMENT CHECKLIST
▼

As you think about board development, consider making use of the following:

1. The process of identifying and recruiting new board members

2. The orientation program for new board members

3. A board self-assessment process that enables the board to comment on the strengths and weaknesses of its own performance

4. A periodic review of the mission statement

5. Special board training workshops on topics such as fund-raising, planning, and financial statements

6. A well-planned discussion on a facet of the board's work, such as the committee structure, the content and conduct of board meetings, or how to increase board diversity

7. Presentations by outside consultants or staff experts on trends in the organization's mission area or community

8. A well-planned and carefully scheduled retreat

9. Special governance workshops offered by local and national management assistance providers

SUGGESTED RESOURCES

Axelrod, Nancy R. *The Chief Executive's Role in Developing the Nonprofit Board.* Washington, DC: National Center for Nonprofit Boards, 1988, 16 pages.

This booklet, the second in NCNB's Nonprofit Governance Series, focuses on the chief executive's role in board development. It outlines eight key responsibilities, including ensuring that job descriptions are in place, helping the board maintain an effective nominating committee, and keeping the board informed.

Bader, Barry S. *Planning Successful Board Retreats: A Guide for Board Members and Chief Executives.* Washington, DC: National Center for Nonprofit Boards, 1990, 28 pages.

Includes nuts-and-bolts advice about how to plan a board retreat, along with a planning checklist and a sample pre-retreat questionnaire and agenda.

Chait, Richard P. *How to Help Your Board Govern More and Manage Less.* Washington, DC: National Center for Nonprofit Boards, 1993, 16 pages.

An examination of the reasons why some boards tend to manage more than govern, followed by an explanation of the role of the board and the chief executive and suggestions on how the two can work together to help the board focus on governance.

Houle, Cyril O. *Governing Boards.* Washington, DC: National Center for Nonprofit Boards, 1989, 223 pages.

This comprehensive work includes background information on boards, a thorough discussion of board structure and operations, the complex relationship between board and staff, and an examination of the board's external relationships.

Nelson, Judith Grummon. *Six Keys to Recruiting, Orienting, and Involving Nonprofit Board Members.* Washington, DC: National Center for Nonprofit Boards, 1991, 58 pages.

This step-by-step guide to finding, recruiting, and involving new board members includes more than a dozen forms, worksheets, and checklists that can be copied and shared.

O'Connell, Brian. *The Board Member's Book.* New York: The Foundation Center, 1993, 208 pages.

This newly updated book provides a thorough analysis of the role and responsibilities of boards. Topics covered include board-staff relations, planning, working with committees, Robert's Rules of Order, and evaluating results. The appendix includes a detailed bibliography.

Slesinger, Larry H. *Self-Assessment for Nonprofit Governing Boards.* Washington, DC: National Center for Nonprofit Boards, 1991, 45 pages.

NCNB's self-assessment instrument includes a questionnaire for board members and a facilitator's guide. The questionnaire is built around 11 basic board responsibilities and is designed to assess board members' satisfaction at how well the board as a whole and each member individually are fulfilling those responsibilities.

ABOUT THE AUTHOR

Maureen K. Robinson is director of education for the National Center for Nonprofit Boards. Since her appointment in 1990, she has supervised the management of NCNB's Board Information Center, board development program, workshops, and conferences. Prior to joining NCNB, Ms. Robinson recruited museum directors for the Smithsonian Institution and served as legislative coordinator for the American Association of Museums. As NCNB's director of education, she has worked with hundreds of nonprofit organizations to create board development programs.